SACRED

Children's choir (or S1) and SATB unaccompanied

OXFORD

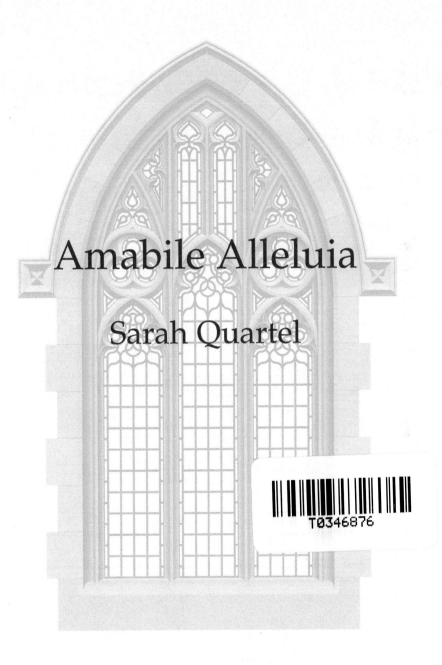

Amabile Alleluia

Sarah Quartel

T0346876

MUSIC DEPARTMENT

OXFORD
UNIVERSITY PRESS

Commissioned by the Amabile Choirs of London, Canada, with funding from the Westminster College Foundation; dedicated to Jackie Norman, Wendy Landon, and the Amabile Choirs in celebration of the organization's 35th anniversary

Amabile Alleluia

SARAH QUARTEL

* In the absence of a children's choir, the sopranos should divide between this part and their given line. Additionally, the children's choir part may be sung by the congregation or audience.

Duration: 2 mins

Music originated by Andrew Jones
Printed in England by Halstan & Co. Ltd, Amersham, Bucks.

ISBN 978-0-19-354408-6